FOOTPRINTS
STILL
Whispering
IN THE WIND

MARGIE TESTERMAN

WHITE DOG PRESS

Table OF CONTENTS

Dedication

I wish to dedicate this book to my loving parents, who instilled in me a sense of pride in who I was and what I could accomplish. By thoughts, deeds, and love, they always made me aware of my Chickasaw heritage.

Margie Testerman

Acknowledgements

This book of poems is a dream come true for me, made possible by the love of my parents, brothers, and children. With their encouragement, I want to pass on my legacy to future generations. As a child I was afforded knowledge of my heritage and developed a reverence for the natural world—a respect I try to convey in my writing. May this book serve as a memorial to all those who came before, especially my parents. The footprints of my ancestors cannot be erased by any modern invention, and their commitment to our people and culture will not be forgotten. My thanks to the Chickasaw children whose illustrations brought my poems to life. My thanks also to the staff of the White Dog Press, whose encouragement and efforts provided an experience I will always cherish.

Margie Testerman

About
MARGIE TESTERMAN

F ootprints Still Whispering in the Wind is Margie Testerman's first published collection of poetry after writing for more than three decades. Her work is inspired by her desire to share the strength, beauty, and grace of her Native American heritage.

Margie and her brothers James, Buddy, John Jr., and Richard grew up in Cushing, Oklahoma, during the 1930s and '40s. She recalls the influences of her Chickasaw ancestry and the culture of the Sac and Fox tribe, many of whose members lived in the area. She recounts how, as a child, she attended Sac and Fox powwows and events, and collected Native American-inspired jewelry from local shops when she could.

After she graduated from Cushing High School in 1950, where she sang in the choir and served on the school newspaper and yearbook staffs, Margie married Bill Quick, and the two began their family.

Bill died suddenly in 1972, and Margie, who had been working from home as a seamstress, sought a way to support herself and her four children, David, Ronnie, CeAnn, and Randy.

She took a job as a teacher's aide at a local school, and managed to fit in a few classes for herself, including a literature class at the local vocational school.

Motivated by her experience, the need to provide for her then college-age children, and the encouragement of her co-workers and instructors, Margie entered college at forty-one.

With hard work and dedication, Margie earned high marks and honors, including the dean's honor roll, before graduating with a bachelor's degree in education in 1977. She accepted a teaching position with Agra public schools, where she taught fifth grade, met and married John Testerman, and went on to earn a master's degree in education in 1984. She retired in 1993.

During that time, she began writing poetry.

Much of her work features Native American themes, including removal, but she also has composed tributes to two brothers she lost to cancer. In recent years, Margie's work has turned toward themes including nature, dance, and childhood memories, as featured in this collection.

Margie also is an avid artist, loves to travel, and has visited landmarks across the globe. She currently lives in Cushing, and is active in a number of civic and professional organizations there.

Opening

FOOTPRINTS STILL WHISPERING IN THE WIND

The far-off mountains hide you from me.
The forests of mighty oaks
Are gone from the naked eye.
Skyscrapers dot the horizon,
Where our homes used to be.
Footprints still whispering in the wind.

We who traveled to distant lands
Walked in soft prints,
Now we walk in moccasins
that mark the earth with
deep prints. Oh! Mother
Earth where is your voice?
Footprints still whispering in the wind.

A mighty rumbling shook the earth.
From within the native hut,
the sound stirred the dusk.
Cyclones roamed the earth
touching the face of destiny
untamed by God's hand.
Footprints still whispering in the wind.

The children of the past at the
break of day, saw rivers
of silver, lost in the morning mist.
Now see the dazzling glare of
iron and steel. Mighty as the
night where nothing stood, now
stand the haughty bridges.
Footprints still whispering in the wind.

Poems
OF NATURE AND BEAUTY

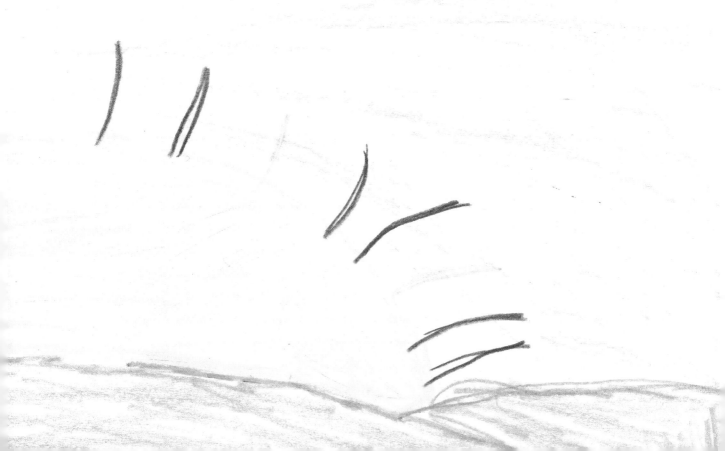

REMEMBER ME

The dawn says awaken
Flowers nodding in the sun
While the sun blazes the hills
Even the wind sighs and soothes
Hills echo the winds
The river gurgles and laughs
Birds are whistling and singing
Raindrops chortle with joy
The sky becomes your canopy
Remember me says the sparrow

TWEET TWEET

At the onset of dawn
Why do birds sing
    The dawn's cool yellow and orange
    Send them on search by wing.

The morning a challenge
Cool grass wet with dew
    Flower heads hung low
    To the bird morning is new.

Searching for forage
With sharp eyes they look
    Dipping and skimming
    In crannies and nook.

Little ones in a nest
Hatchlings nestled in a row
    Mouths open in anticipation
    Mom sees and dips low.

In their mouth she finds
Dad swoops in to check
    Chicks chirp with glee
    Mom and Dad both at beck.

Mom flies off to eat
It's Dad's turn to sit
    With food in his mouth
    He sits down for a bit.

Soon Mom flies home
Both Mom and Dad fed
    The little ones settle down
    Soon sleep in the bed.

Shadows are lengthening
With heads nestled under wing
    Little ones are settled
    This is why birds sing.

Artwork by Lauren John, age 11

Kaitlyn Tingle

THE FEATHER

What are you seeking?
have you been to a dance
　　you wind and waft
the air your buffet
　　twirling and curling
caught by the current
　　circles you make aloft.

Will you land in a nest?
or on a rail fence
　　the wind sighs and says come
you flit and prance
　　to the meadow you go
you swoop and bend
　　the wind says follow.

Do you see the clouds?
high in the blue sky
　　come and drift they say
the earth beckons and calls
　　the current sighs and sends
each bent on their call
　　the feather drifts in leisure.

Artwork by Kaitlyn Tingle, age 13　11

INDIAN PAINTBRUSH

Blazing colors that dot the horizon,
As far as the eye can see.
Dancing colors waving aimlessly.

Bringing hope and vision of spring
As the colors deck the hillside
Down in the valleys and lees.

Bold colors of red and orange,
Matching the warriors' painted faces,
Enliven the hearts of many.

The Indian paintbrush flowers
Herald the spring with color
As far as the eye can see.

HARVEST

We planted the seeds
The plants sprang up
　　They met our needs.

The pumpkins did grow
Twirling and vining
　　Grow in a row.

Fixed in a dish
Squash great and small
　　For all to relish.

Corn stored in a bin
Waiting to be a meal
　　For kith and kin.

The pecans did fall
To be stored, put away
　　Enjoyed by one and all.

Harvest came and went
We now wait for spring
　　What our hopes will bring.

MARCH OF THE LEAVES

Watch the hustle and bustle of leaves
All decked out in gold and brown
Marching like little soldiers
Some in bib and some in gown.

The wind their commander and chief
Halting, then marching down the street
Turning and swaying with a salute
Twisting and saluting whom they meet.

Artwork by Jesse Clark, age 11

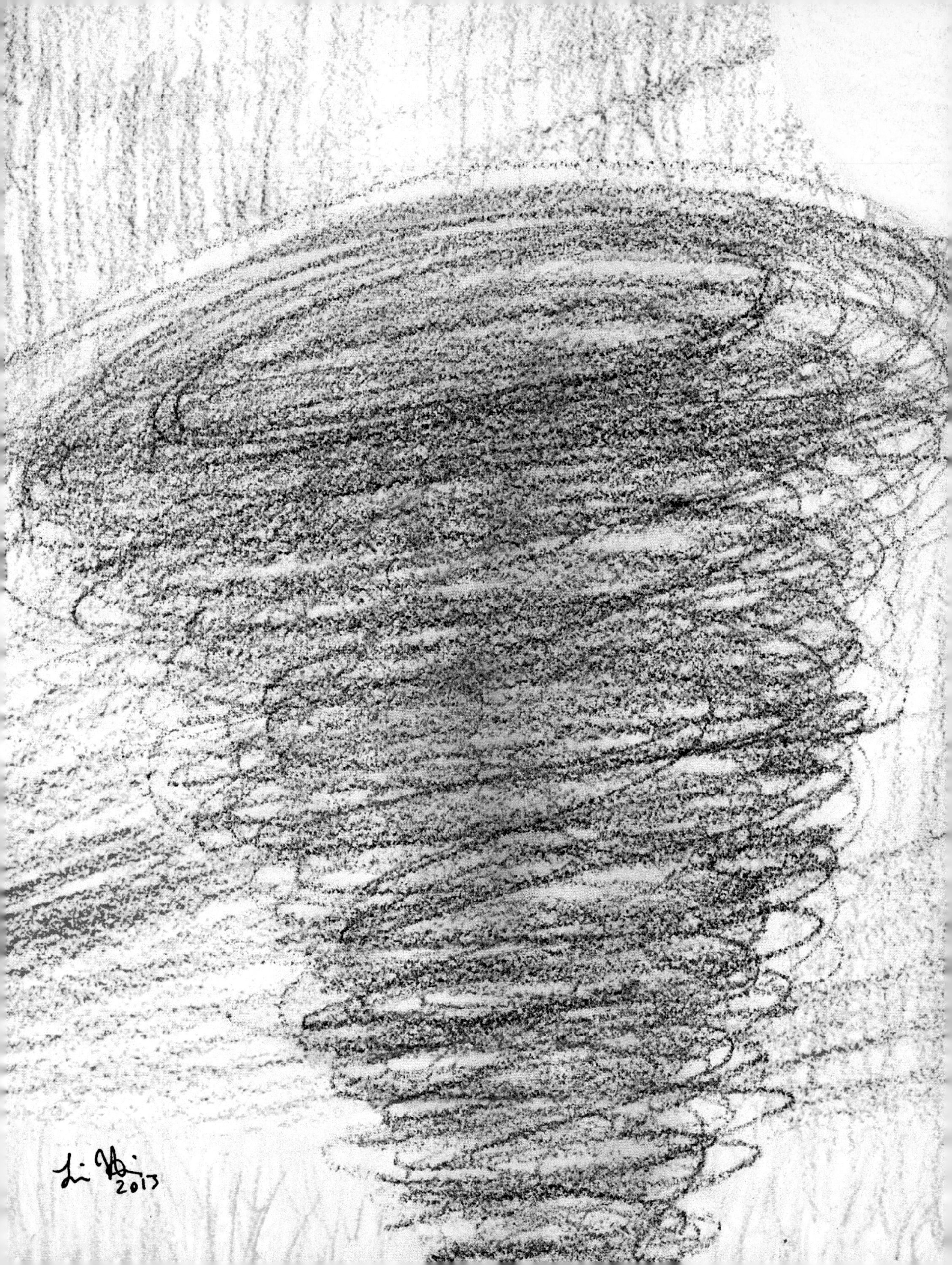
2013

THE WHIRLWIND

The whirlwind dances and blows
   dips high and bends low.

The dust devil is circling
   in a cloud of brown mist.

Whirls in a dervish bow
   twirling and prancing.

Windblown circles low
   in wonderment we watch.

Specks of dancing dust
   clouding our view.

Movements soon gone
   as the whirlwind dances and blows.

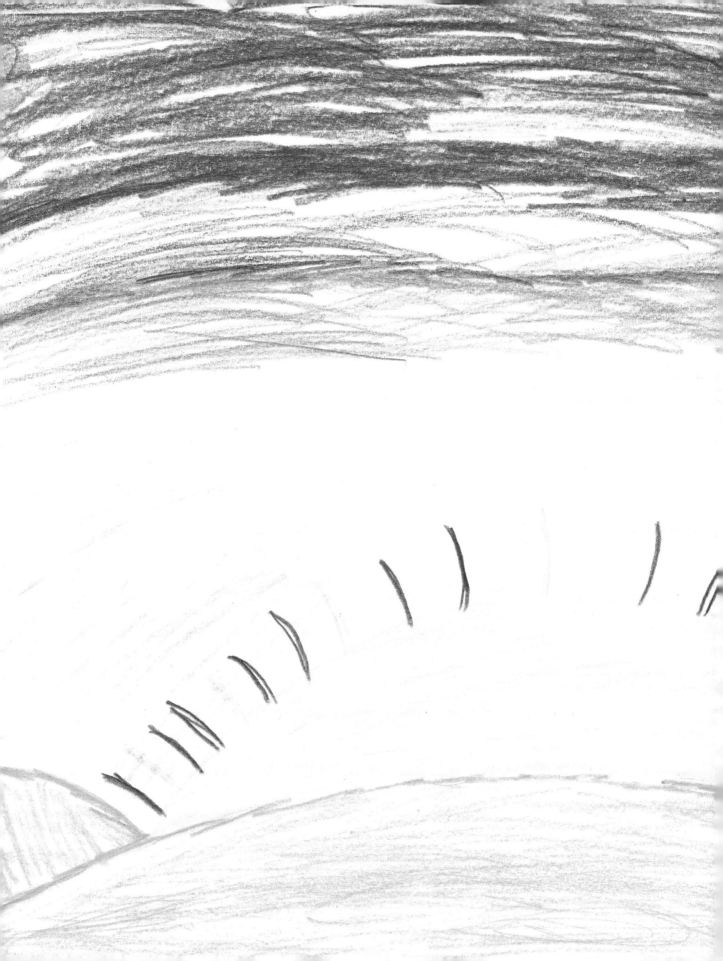

TWILIGHT

Twilight comes creeping on lowly feet.
Stealing throbs of the drum's beat.

Shadows dancing among campfires.
Swaying to voices of the criers.

The drum heralds the twilight.
Harkening to the dancer's might.

Feathers casting shadows of dance.
Eerie shapes of the warriors prance.

When nighttime calls the old one.
To sing chants of victories won.

Silently stealing catching the beat.
Twilight comes creeping on lowly feet.

Artwork by Lauren John, age 11 21

CRY OF THE WOLF

On a lonesome hill he stands
Silhouetted in the moonlight.

All four feet on watch
Looking for his mate.

His mournful cry a prayer
He who knows the blackness of night.

Waiting for his mate to return
In the den his little ones sleep.

Watchful eyes surveying
 His cry sung with might.

In the valley and mountain high
The hills echo his cry.

Artwork by Macen Marris, age 10

THE MOON

The moon lights our path
    and guides our way.

When the moon hovers
    squirrels chase and bark.

The raccoon stealthy walks
    while the deer crush leaves.

Owls watch from a limb
    the beaver watches with disdain.

A full moon peers over trees
    the bobcat leaps and jumps.

Spiders creep and crawl
    while blowing leaves sing songs.

Poems
OF SONG AND DANCE

I LISTEN WITH MY HEART

When the leaves sing in the wind,
    Birds trilling at break of dawn.

Flowers nodding with each tune,
    When the trees bow and bend.

I hear the earth singing,
    Then I listen with my heart.

When the prairie grass is bent,
    The birds' wings sing a sonnet.

Creeks and rivers ripple verses,
    Songs and singing were meant.

Then I listen with my heart,
    When the cicadas whisper low.

The birds echo each refrain,
    Drums and flutes dance with each beat.

Leaves flutter with the wind's blow,
    Then I listen with my heart.

Artwork by Faithlyn Seawright, age 15 **29**

I SING A SONG

I sing a song
From the tales of my elders
    Why leaves sing of honor
When birds' wings weave the notes
    Oh! Mother Earth thy love
Is endless with the seasons
    Melodies waft on breezes
The crickets sing of dreams
    Not set to notes on leaves
When I sing, I remember.

Artwork by Maryanne Criswell, age 8   31

SING DANCE

Feathers in the victory dance,
Singing dance dance.

While the embers are whispering,
singing dance dance.

Drummers beating to a chant,
singing dance dance.

Footsteps stepping to a chant,
singing dance dance.

The victorious warriors are,
singing dance dance.

Singers chanting cheering,
singing dance dance.

Artwork by Micah Postoak, age 9

A MAIDEN'S SONG

Hear me, I dance to a beat
    of a warrior's drum. Sing! Sing!
Hear me, my turtle shells shake
    as my legs dance. Sing! Sing!
Hear me, the pebbles shout
    they rattle, shake, move. Sing! Sing!
Hear me, the embers blaze
    dancers move the wind. Sing! Sing!
Hear me, I dance in glee
    the warriors victorious. Sing! Sing!
Hear me, the dancers say to all
    happy are the victors. Sing! Sing!

Artwork by Faithlyn Seawright, age 15

TURTLE DANCE

To a young maiden
Dancing the turtle dance
Legs shaking in rhythm
While the turtle shells shake
River pebbles resounding
As they did in the riverbed
Dancing to honor the turtle.

Gives joy to each dancer
Legs shake and prance
The maiden follows a rhythm
A sound the pebbles make
The turtle dance gives pride
As the maiden shakes her head
When the evening dusk nears.

Artwork by T.J. Clark, age 13

THE DANCE BEGINS

The dance begins
    to celebrate the cry
        of the young babe.
His name is sung to
    the beat of the drum.

The dance begins
    to honor the sun.
Its rays warm the
    heart of the earth
        and soul of man.

The dance begins,
    victory has been won.
The warrior's honor
    bespeaks his courage
        and badge of pride.

The dance begins,
    the marriage feast prepared.
to join hearts of the young
    warrior and maiden in
        dreams of eternity.

GREEN CORN DANCE

Around the dancing embers
Feathers flowing with the wind.
Legs throbbing with each beat,
As the drums' messages send.

Hearts and souls celebrate
Thanksgiving of harvests born.
The mighty winter forestalled,
With the gathering of corn.

The Green Corn Dance,
Feathers float and bend,
Celebrates victory over hunger,
While the dancers' messages send.

I SING

I sing to the gossamer moon
I sing to the willow tree
I sing to the evening loon
I sing to be happy.

I sing to the goldenrod
I sing to the gurgling brook
I sing to the rain-soaked sod
I sing to be happy.

I sing to the shallow pond
I sing to the shining stars
I sing to the lilies donned
I sing to be happy.

I sing to the clouds of blue
I sing to the rolling hills
I sing to the rainbow hue
I sing to be happy.

Artwork by Noah Hinson, age 8

WHEN ALONE, WE DANCE

When alone, we dance
to the shrill of the whistle.
We twist and turn matching
the cricket's din.

When alone, we dance
to the whirring of the wind.
Trying to catch the matchless
whirlwind's prancing and pivoting.

When alone, we dance
to the ripples of streams passing.
Knowing only the rocks sense
our movement and cheer.

When alone, we dance
to the sigh of the trees.
As the leaves chortle
and its branches whisper.

When alone, we dance
while the meadows sing.
The blades of grass matching
the swaying of our arms.

When alone, we dance
to the wildflowers bending.
With movement matching
the rhythm of our hands.

When alone, we dance
to the beat of the Earth's heart.
Ever turning, searching
for the soul of each throb.

Artwork by Chelsea Wedlow, age 13 45

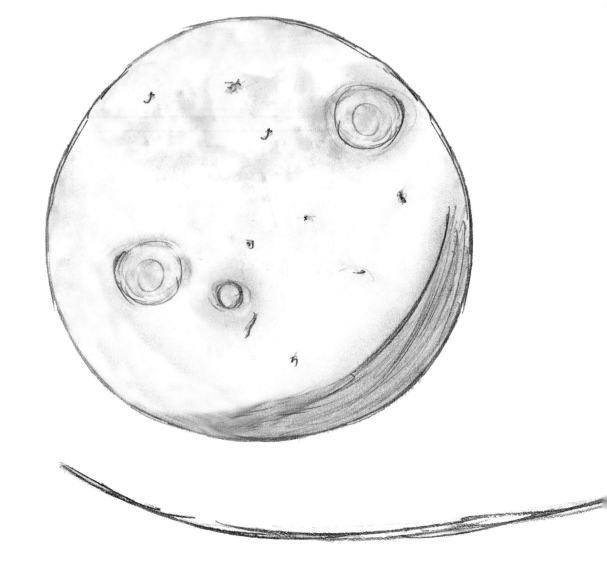

Poems
OF PEACE AND COMFORT

Peace

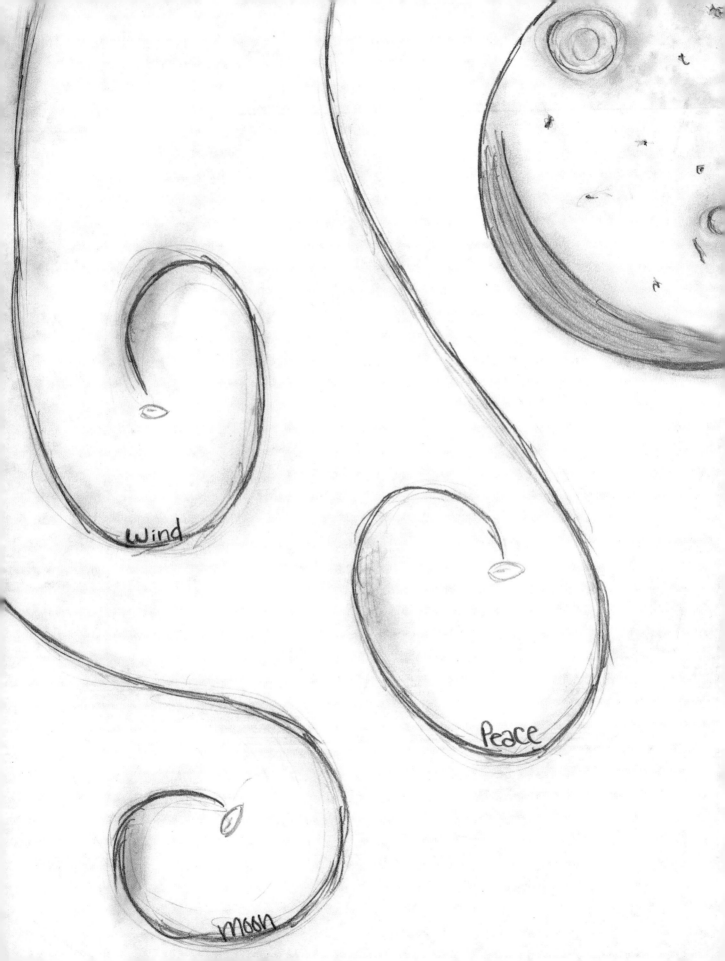

WHEN THE WIND SPEAKS

Hear the leaves whisper
    while the wind coos and calls.

In the wind I imagine music
    and the sound of voices.

Gentle sighs catch my ears
    while the wind soothes souls.

Blowing wind filters the moon
    while circlets fall on the ground.

The silence of the wind
    brings quiet and peace.

We listen with anticipation
    when the wind speaks.

FREEDOM AND MAJESTY

The restless undaunted eagle
    over the hills and valleys

In search of a dream
    The sky his realm

Treetops his home
    Dipping, swooping, lifting

Eyes darting, wings fluttering
    He who knows freedom

Finding solace in the sky
    As the eagle flies boldly

Seeking, searching, listing
    Surveying the sky

The sky fulfills his dream
    With freedom and majesty

Artwork by T.J. Clark, age 13

SPIRIT WATERS

The spirit waters, Earth's dress
Touching her whole realm
How you nourish Mother Earth
Little drops from the sky, little spirits
You fall bringing the little spirits
You trickle, splash, and cavort
Lakes meander in joyful song
Streams whisper, rivers chortle
How raindrops dance in glee
Filling lakes, streams, and rivers.
Children splash in the pools
Fresh air cleansed by your fall
Mother Earth is dressed in green
Spirit waters, God's handiwork.

WALKING IN THE WOODS

Twigs crunching under foot
　While walking in the woods
　　Peaceful are the sounds
　　　Sunlit rays filtering trees

The soul finds solace
　In the coo of the quail
　　Scratching the forest floor
　　　Wild turkeys shout free

Leaves dance in the wind
　Brambles catch one's legs
　　The trillium flowers abound
　　　Down the valley and lee

The wind whispers softly
　Moccasin steps not heard
　　Peace floods the soul
　　　My heart says free

PEACE TO THE SOUL

The twigs under foot crunch
Light filters making circlets
The trillium blossoms nod hello
Water gurgling breaks silence.
    Brings peace to the soul.

The wood ferns sing a song
Shadows broken by clouds movement
The cardinal dips and dives
His color lifts the heart.
    Brings peace to the soul.

Solace broken by the crow's call
Trees standing like soldiers
Each bidding come
Leaves dropping in silence.
    Bring peace to the soul.

WE ARE NEVER ALONE

We are never alone when
the stars guide us and
provide the bountiful hope
of a new dawning morn.

The warming sun rays
thrill our beings with
watchful eyes of the
unfolding of shafts of corn.

The caroling cries of
the wind cools our
burning skin in the
deep of summer's heat.

The windswept rain
brings hope to the
fields of grain and faith
in the unfolding of seasons.

The hills provide watchful
eyes to see beyond
the ebb of time.
We are never alone.

YOU'LL SEE

I saw the wind in the leaves
as they danced to and fro.
      You'll see

Red, yellow, and orange leaves
Gracefully drifting to the ground.
      You'll see

The snow their blanket
Awaiting spring's call.
      You'll see

The trees budding signals wake
while tiny buds emerge.
      You'll see

What God has created
will restore in glory and splendor.
      You'll see

All seasons work together
for the beauty of the earth.
      You'll see

I AM

I am a flower beside the road
I am a tree who sings a song
I am the wind in the hills
I see the four corners of the world
I am the sun who gives warmth
I am a little chick who says peep
I am the stars who wink
I am a soaring eagle
I am a feather floating leisurely
I am the glitter in the snow
I am the drip drip of the rain
I am a deer standing in the woods
I am a rabbit who hops in play
I am a opossum who forages
I made the blue in the sky
I made the green in the grass
I made the moon yellow
I am the clouds who dot the sky
I am the star who lights the way
I am the dusk who harkens
I am the ebony night
I am the Great Spirit in the sky.

Artwork by Trevor John, age 8

MOCCASIN TRAILS

Through the trees
Twigs snapping, leaves bending,
ever touching the wind.
Gently moving the limbs,
trees trapping the sounds.
Moccasin trails

Over streams
Water lapping, trilling sounds
moving over mossy rocks.
Going on ever and ever
thoughtless of mapping footprints.
Moccasin trails

The hills beyond
echo unspoken sounds.
Lapping against craggy crevices,
unmindful of blowing winds.
The lowly hills whisper
Moccasin trails

The fields abound
with blossoms of paintbrushes
filling the sleeping valleys.
Mapping the trails with leaves
crushed underfoot, undaunted by
Moccasin trails

ODE TO THE CREATOR

The mountains appear as monuments,
Great is the Father who fashioned.

In the shadows your voice,
Speaks with the approach of dusk.

I will forever lift mine eyes,
As the stars in the clouds whisper.

My heart moves with the leaves,
Joy stirs the chords of love.

The river sings your praises,
Talking rocks echo the refrain.

I sing with voices of the birds,
My songs will glorify thee.

The rain quiets the murmurs,
As the gentle nodding flowers toll.

Though I walk in moccasins,
My footsteps follow thee.

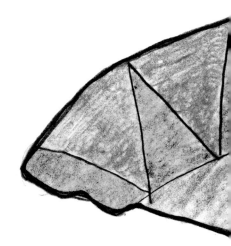

Artwork by Chelsea Wedlow, age 13

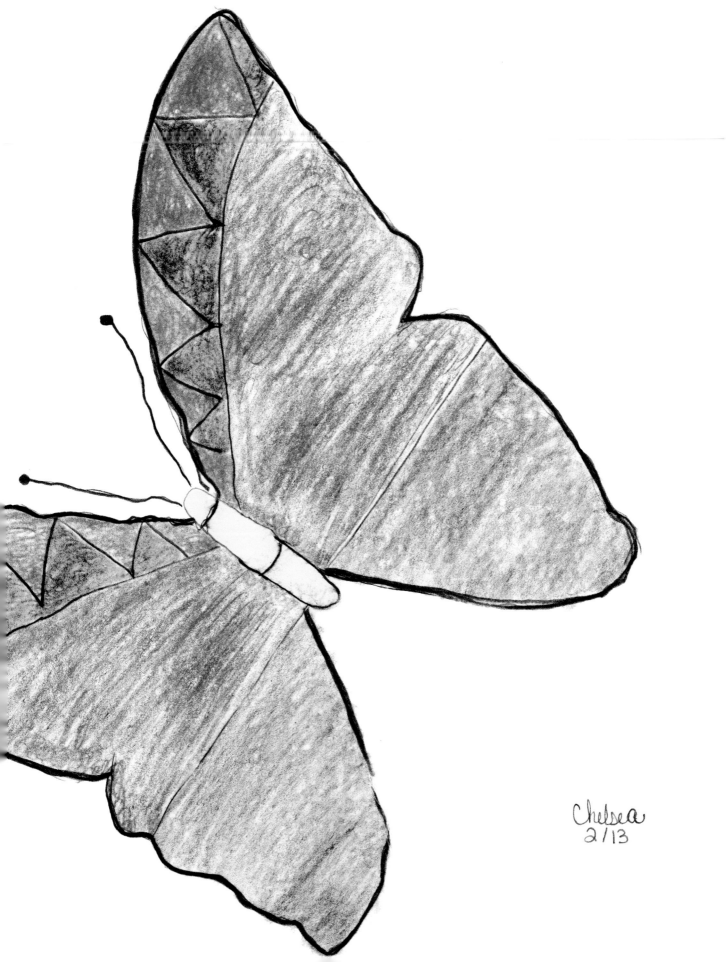

Closing

MY STORY, MY SONG

I sing to the blue sky
Shadow of the yucca listens
The rocks hear me and cheer.

I sing to the tall pines
The lilies in the valley whisper
Ripples in the river sigh.

I sing to the sleeping babe
Switch grass nods in agreement
While the hills speak freedom.

I sing to the sunlit meadow
The mountains speak to the moon
Leaves swing to the breeze.

I sing to shaking turtle shells
My moccasined feet chant
Feathers like notes float in the wind.

I sing to the Great Spirit
Who hears your prayers
This is my story, my song.

Artwork by Jordan Stick, age 14